PLANET EARTH

WEATHER AND CLIMATE

George and Anne Purvis

The Bookwright Press
New York · 1984

PLANET EARTH

Coastlines
Volcanoes
The Oceans
Water on the Land
The Work of the Wind
Weather and Climate

First published in the United States in 1984 by
The Bookwright Press, 387 Park Avenue South,
New York, NY 10016

First published in 1983 by
Wayland (Publishers) Ltd
49 Lansdowne Place, Hove
East Sussex BN3 1HF, England

ISBN 0-531-04788-1

Library of Congress Catalog Card Number 83-72798

Printed in Italy by
G. Canale & C.S.p.A., Turin

Contents

A bright but cold winter's day in Greenland.

Aspects of the weather

"Weather" is something we are all familiar with—a sunny day, a frosty night, or a thunderstorm. But for some people "weather" can mean life or death. The **tornadoes** of the North American plains and the **hurricanes** of the Caribbean and China seas are examples. For others, the absence of some eagerly-awaited weather might spell disaster. The failure of the Indian **monsoon** rains to appear on schedule can trigger off famine and drought affecting millions.

Unfortunately, it is usually bad weather that gets noticed. In February 1983 the record snowstorms in the northeastern states of the U.S.A. and the devastating firestorms in southern Australia both hit the headlines.

Just from these few examples, we can see that weather appears in a bewildering variety of guises. Indeed, in an area as small as the British Isles, the changes in the weather on a single day can be difficult to catalog in detail. At the other extreme, there are vast areas of the Earth, such as the permanent deserts, where the weather is virtually the same, day after day, year after year.

But it is not only the Earth that has weather—some of the other planets in our solar system have their own, very different weather systems, and sometimes we can understand the Earth's weather better if we study the behavior of the atmospheres of other planets.

By looking at these and other aspects of the weather, this book provides an insight into the fascinating way our atmosphere works.

Drought may spell disaster for crops and livestock.

The atmosphere

Where did the air we breathe come from? It is now believed that when the Earth was first formed, about 4,500 million years ago, it had no atmosphere. The atmosphere developed later as a result of volcanic activity. When the Earth was very young, it had many more volcanoes than exist today. They were also much larger, more violent and much more active. The enormous quantity of hot gases which were ejected from these volcanoes provided the raw materials which evolved, over millions of years, into the mixture of gases in the atmosphere today.

Not all young volcanic planets develop atmospheres though. The moon was once such a planet, yet today it has no atmosphere. Being a small planet, it had insufficient **gravity** to prevent its new atmosphere from leaking away into space.

A satellite photo of the swirling clouds in the Earth's atmosphere.

What the atmosphere is made of

The Earth's atmosphere is a mixture of gases, mainly nitrogen and oxygen, with traces of other gases.

Another name for a gas is vapor (*atmos* is Greek for vapor), which means water vapor is a gas. In terms of weather, water vapor is the most important gas in the air, although there is very little of it compared with oxygen and nitrogen. It is water vapor that gives us our rain, hail, clouds, and snow.

Gases in the Atmosphere

Gas	Quantity
Nitrogen	78%
Oxygen	21%
Argon	0.01%
Water vapor—up to	0.04%

There are also traces of carbon dioxide, neon, helium, krypton, hydrogen and ozone.

There is also very little carbon dioxide or ozone in the atmosphere, but their effects are also important. Carbon dioxide is a colorless, odorless gas, which has an indirect effect on the weather. It traps the heat radiated from the sun-warmed Earth. The Earth would be much cooler if there were no carbon dioxide. Ozone also traps heat in the atmosphere, but this happens very high up, about 30 to 50 km up (18.5 to 31 miles), in the **ozone layer**. More important, the ozone layer shields us from the harmful burning effects of the sun's **ultra-violet** radiation.

The Earth's atmosphere doesn't really have a top; it just merges into space. For our purposes though, we can consider the atmosphere to have two layers. The lower is called the **troposphere** (which means "sphere of change") and it extends upwards to about 8 km (5 miles) at the north and south poles, and about 16 km (10 miles) at the **equator.** All our weather takes place in the troposphere. Roughly speaking, if the Earth were an apple, the troposphere would only be as thick as the skin. Above the troposphere is the upper atmosphere or **stratosphere.**

Seen from space, the atmosphere appears as a thin blue haze.

Atmospheric temperature and pressure

The atmosphere's temperature gets colder the higher you go. Where the temperature at the surface is 20°C (68°F), it will be about -30°C (-22°F) at a height of 5 km (8 miles).

The temperature will continue to fall steadily until you reach the top of the troposphere, known as the tropopause. Beyond the tropopause is the stratosphere, where the temperature remains the same for a while but then begins to rise steadily as you go higher and approach the warm ozone layer.

Not only does temperature decrease with height, it also decreases as you approach the north and south poles. The reason for this is that at the equator the sun is almost directly overhead, whereas at the poles the sun is always low in the sky. The sun's rays therefore strike the poles at an angle and so are spread over a wider area. You can get an idea of what happens by shining a flashlight on the ceiling. Shone directly overhead, you see a bright concentrated spotlight, but if you tilt the flashlight, the spotlight spreads out and becomes less intense. Also, because of their angle, the sun's rays must pass through a greater thickness of atmosphere at the poles, which also weakens them. This is why you can look directly at the sun when it is on

Mount Kenya in Africa is tall enough to be snow-capped all year.

the horizon—at this time the atmosphere between your eyes and the sun is at its thickest. You cannot do this, and must never try, when the sun is high in the sky—it will damage your eyes.

The weight of the atmosphere is something we are not aware of, although it is constantly pressing down on us. It presses equally from every direction, which is why we don't notice it. In fact, it presses very hard—a rubber suction pad, for example, sticks to a smooth surface because of the weight of atmospheric pressure.

Atmospheric pressure is measured by a barometer. The readings that a modern barometer gives are in millibars (mb for short). At the Earth's surface the barometer will on average read 1000mb. At the top of the troposphere the pressure will be about 120mb, or roughly one tenth of what it is at the surface. The rule is that the higher you go, the lower the pressure will be. The atmosphere also becomes thinner the higher you go—when the atmosphere finally merges into space, the pressure is zero. On very high mountains, climbers have to carry oxygen cylinders because there is not enough oxygen in the thin air.

You can safely look at the sun when it is setting.

The wind

Many of the Earth's winds depend upon the simple rule that warm air rises. If some cold air is warmed up, it expands, becoming less dense, and it rises—rather like a cork released from the bottom of a water tank. While this warmed air rises, the surrounding air will flow in to replace it. The result is a circulation called **convection**. If convection continues for long enough, an area of **low pressure** will result beneath the rising air and a corresponding **high pressure** area will develop beneath the sinking air.

A sea breeze is caused by convection.

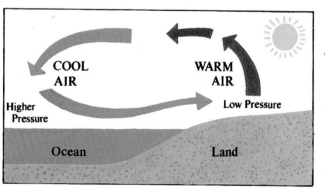

Sea breezes

A common feature of coastlines is the sea breeze. This develops on calm sunny days when air over the land is warmed faster than over the sea. The air over the land rises, and is replaced by the cooler sea air. At night the land cools faster than the sea, and an opposite, but weaker, land breeze develops.

Sea breezes are stronger and penetrate further inland in the tropics than in cooler temperate areas because the temperature difference between the sea and land is greater.

Indian monsoon winds

The central plains of India are heated intensely in the summer months of March to June. The air over the plains rises, drawing the air over the Indian Ocean inland, as a very moist southwesterly airstream. This is the wet summer monsoon. The reverse happens in winter, when the sea is warmer than the land, and then a dry northeasterly monsoon

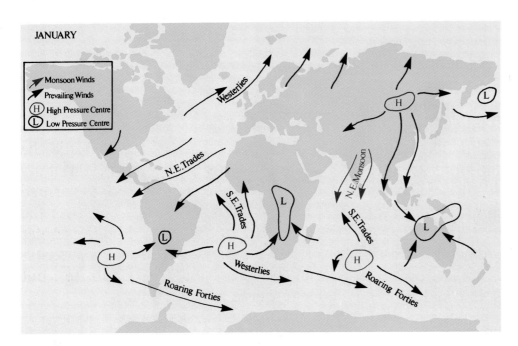

Left *The plains cool down by January, and dry wind blows back across the ocean.*

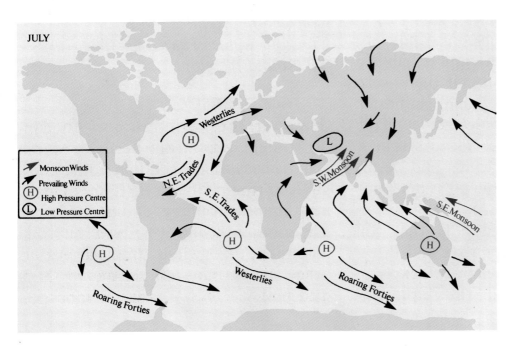

Left *In July, the wet summer monsoon blows over the central plains of India.*

develops. Monsoon winds are really sea and land breezes, but they happen on an immense scale.

The arrival of the summer monsoon generates frequent, violent thunderstorms, and torrential rain. The steamy and uncomfortable conditions are ideal for the rapid growth of weeds and mildew, and much more important, food crops. However, the arrival is sudden and fairly unpredictable. If the summer monsoon rains are late or intermittent, the crops will fail and famine may result.

Global winds

Sea breezes and monsoon winds are examples of Nature's attempt to balance extremes of temperature. If there were no winds, the equator would get hotter and hotter, and the poles colder. This doesn't happen because Nature sets up a global circulation of winds and ocean currents which warm the poles and cool the equator (see page 11).

The natural tendency is that air warmed at the equator rises and flows poleward, to be replaced by colder polar air flowing toward the equator.

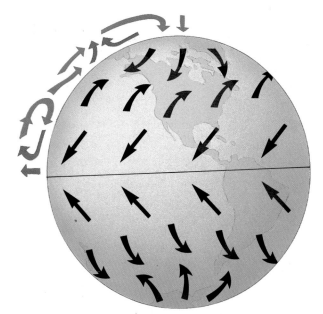

The top left-hand corner shows how convection produces the world's constant winds. The same effect works all around the globe.

However, the moving air does not flow in straight lines from north to south. This is because the rotation of the Earth deflects the moving air (to the right in the northern hemisphere, and to the left in the southern), and it is this effect that organizes the winds into large-scale weather systems of low and high pressure.

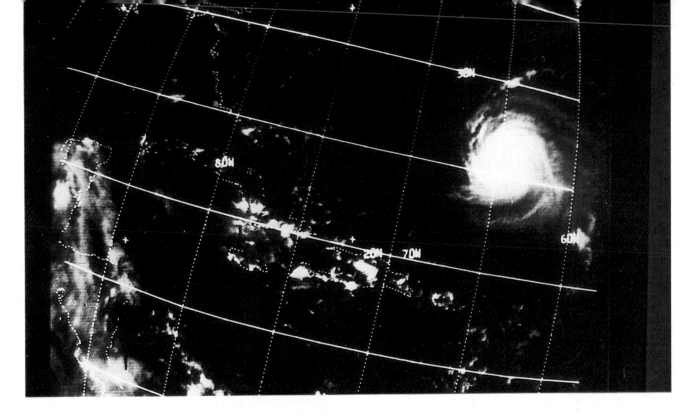

A satellite picture showing the dense cloud of a hurricane (top right) spiraling counterclockwise in the northern hemisphere.

Hurricanes

Only a tiny proportion of the population experiences hurricanes, yet most of us know they are winds of extraordinary power. A hurricane is a region of wind and cloud violently spiraling into an intense low pressure center at ground level, and out again at higher levels. It is a whirlpool of the atmosphere, which always revolves counterclockwise in the northern hemisphere and clockwise in the southern. The center of a hurricane, known as the eye, is relatively calm and cloud-free.

A hurricane is usually 1,000 kilometers wide (620 miles), and about 7 kilometers high (4.3 miles). The highest wind speeds are found in a narrow band circling the eye, where they can reach more than 190 k.p.h. (120 m.p.h.). Hurricanes normally move quite slowly along a fairly predictable path, although they may wobble, like a spinning top, up to 100 kilometers (60 miles) to either side of it, or even go into reverse. Hurricanes get their energy from the sea, and they usually begin to weaken once they hit land, but for reasons not yet understood, some do not.

The causes of hurricanes are complex, but they begin when giant thunderstorms, generated over a warm tropical sea, cluster together in just the right arrangement. The greatest of these hurricanes occur over the China Sea, where they are known as typhoons. Hurricanes of the Indian Ocean are known as tropical cyclones, as are the hurricanes which strike the coasts of Australia.

Tornadoes and whirlwinds

Tornadoes are small, intense whirling tubes of wind embedded in violent thunderstorms, or near the center of hurricanes. They occur most frequently in the midwestern states of the United

Immense thunderclouds form a tornado storm front over West Kansas.

States, between central Texas and the Dakotas. No wind recorder can withstand the impact of a tornado, but the windspeed has been estimated at around 320 k.p.h. (400 m.p.h.).

Tornadoes bump along the ground, hopping aloft, and traveling beneath a black funnel-shaped cloud. Some of the funnels are like pillars, others are snake-like, when the effect is rather like the twitching tail of a rat. Immense damage is caused wherever the tornado strikes the ground—the suction caused by the intense low pressure at the core has been known to pluck the feathers from a chicken! The area of destruction varies from a few feet to a mile, and although sometimes a small town may be flattened and many people killed, an adjacent area can escape damage entirely if the tornado bumps aloft.

Less violent than the land tornadoes are the waterspouts formed over the sea. They too can be destructive if they cross land, but they quickly collapse.

Whirlwinds originate from local surface heating—the rising upcurrents spiral into a vortex. They are usually short-lived but can cause damage. Dust devils and water devils are small whirlwinds named after the debris they carry.

A tornado hits the ground, sucking sand and debris high into the air.

Katabatic winds

On calm nights, the air near the ground cools and becomes heavier. On mountain slopes this air will slide downhill. This is called a **katabatic** or down-slope wind. The katabatic winds which plunge off the Greenland and Antarctic ice caps can exceed 240 k.p.h. (150 m.p.h.).

A weaker **anabatic** or up-slope wind develops on a sunny slope during the day, when air, warmed by contact with the slope, rises and is replaced by nearby, cooler air. This usually happens in the early morning.

Katabatic winds causing mountain valley fog.

Clouds, rain and sky

Clouds appear in a bewildering variety of forms, which the casual onlooker may find difficult to tell apart. In fact there are only two basic cloud types: **cumulus**

Cumulus clouds are caused by convection.

or heap clouds, and **stratus** or layer clouds. Cumulus clouds are formed by convection, whereas layer clouds are formed when larger areas of air are lifted. The two types of clouds appear in different sizes and combinations.

The cumulus family

Cumulus clouds are always lumpy and cauliflower-like, with spaces between the clouds. There are three distinct sizes of cumulus: small or fair-weather cumulus; swelling or towering cumulus; and cumulonimbus or thunderclouds.

The stratus family

These clouds appear in layers or sheets across the sky. They are usually only 0.5 to 1 kilometer thick (1,500 to 3,000 feet), but they can be anything from 10 to

Below *Towering cumulus cloud.*

Above *A combination of altostratus and altocumulus clouds.*

1,000 kilometers wide (16 to 1,600 miles). There are three different types of stratus which occur at different heights: low stratus; medium-level layers known as altostratus; and very high cloud called cirrostratus. Stratus clouds that lie on the ground are better known as fog.

Clouds also appear in combinations— we can have heaps *in* layers, or heaps *and* layers. Stratocumulus is an example of a heap in a layer (a sheet of cumulus), and cumulus and altostratus is an example of a heap and a layer.

Above *Smaller cumulus clouds are associated with fair weather.*

Below *This type of cumulus cloud (cumulonimbus) is associated with thunderstorms.*

How clouds form

Clouds form from water vapor—one of the invisible gases in the atmosphere. The amount of water vapor present can vary a great deal, and sometimes there is almost none at all. This dry air will draw up moisture as it passes over water, becoming moist and humid. This is called **evaporation.** The humid air will form clouds if it is cooled below a certain temperature known as the **dewpoint** temperature. Below this point some of the water vapor condenses into liquid water, in the form of millions and millions of tiny droplets. These become visible to us as clouds. On a cold day your breath forms a cloud because the moist air from your lungs is cooled to below its dewpoint. The dewpoint temperature is a measure of how dry the air is—the lower the dewpoint temperature, the drier the air.

The ground can also cool the nearby air to below its dewpoint. If this happens on a calm night, the water vapor close to the ground will condense as dew. If the temperature is below freezing, the dew will appear as hoarfrost. If there is a light breeze, the cold air layer near the ground will mix into the warmer one above it—and if the temperature of this mixed layer is lower than the dewpoint, fog will form. A slightly stronger breeze could lift the fog above the ground, making a sheet of low stratus cloud.

Moist air forced aloft by a mountain or hill may be cooled below its dewpoint, and will also form clouds.

A tree covered in hoarfrost.

Fog lifted by a slight breeze forms a layer of low stratus cloud.

Clouds may also form when warm air rises. On a sunny day, warm bubbles of air called **thermals** float upward. As they rise, the thermals cool at a steady rate. What happens next depends on the air surrounding the thermals. If they become cooler than the surrounding air, they will sink back to the ground. But if the thermals remain warmer than their surroundings, they will continue to rise and to cool—and if they cool below their dewpoint, cumulus clouds will form.

A huge mushroom-shaped cumulonimbus.

Now an important change takes place: if the clouds are still rising, they will cool at a slower rate than before. There is now more chance that they will remain warmer than the surrounding air. This means that the cumulus clouds can grow up to the top of the troposphere, where they spread out like a mushroom. These huge cumulus clouds are cumulonimbus, or thunderclouds.

Precipitation

We know that clouds are composed of millions of tiny water droplets. In order to **precipitate,** or give rain, snow etc., some of the droplets must increase their size a million times or more. According to one theory, ice crystals grow in the cloud until they become large enough to fall out of the cloud as rain, snow, sleet or hail—depending on the temperature. In this case, the cloud tops must be well below 0°C (32°F). Such cold clouds have fuzzy tops, and cumulonimbus with their mushroom-like tops spreading out are typical examples.

The start of the rainy season on a dry African plain.

A second theory explains "warm" rain clouds, that is, clouds whose tops are warmer than freezing point. In this case, the droplets grow by bumping into each other as they fall through the cloud. Eventually the droplets grow large enough to fall out of the cloud as rain. Often both theories are necessary to explain the formation of rain in a cloud.

Precipitating clouds will usually have "nimbus" or "nimbo" somewhere in their name, as in cumulonimbus (a precipitating cumulus) or nimbostratus (a precipitating stratus).

The sky

When sunlight shines through a glass prism, the light is **refracted,** or separated, into the colors of the rainbow. The colors—red, orange, yellow, green, blue, indigo and violet—are known as the **spectrum.** This demonstrates that sunlight is a mixture of all the colors of the rainbow.

Unlike the solid glass prism, the Earth's atmosphere is composed of tiny

At sunrise, red light is reflected by clouds.

invisible **molecules,** which "scatter" the light in all directions. Some of the colors are scattered more than others— colors at the blue end of the spectrum are scattered more than those at the red end. The sky therefore appears blue to us, because we see more blue scattered light than red. Without the atmosphere, the sun would appear as a fiery ball in an inky black sky—which is how the sun appears on the airless moon.

The scattering effect is greatest at sunrise and sunset, when the sun is low in the sky, and shining through a greater thickness of atmosphere. At these times the light that eventually reaches our eyes is mainly red—which is why the sun appears reddened. Any clouds illuminated by the sun at these times will also appear red or pink. It is important to realize that scattering causes the sky to "shine" with a blue light of its own, whereas clouds mainly reflect light—so if the light is red, the clouds appear red.

The rainbow

A raindrop is a little round ball, or sphere, not teardrop-shaped as we imagine. If the sun is low, and shining

Sometimes a faint outer rainbow is visible.

onto a rain shower, or onto fog, the droplets behave like a glass prism, refracting the light and splitting it into the separate colors of the spectrum. Red is refracted the least, and violet the most, which is why a rainbow is red on the outside and violet on the inside. Sometimes you can see a fainter, secondary rainbow, where the order of colors is reversed. The lower the sun is in the sky, the higher the bow will be. At sunrise or sunset, a full half circle may appear. But at noon, when the sun is nearly overhead, no bow will appear.

25

Coronas and haloes

Frequently the moon can be seen shining through a thin veil of cloud. If the cloud is composed of water droplets, a series of colored rings can be seen surrounding the moon, merging into one another. This effect is called a corona, and is caused by the tiny water droplets splitting the light into colored bands.

Ice crystals also bend light, and so when the sun or moon shines through a

Below A veil of ice crystals causes a halo round the moon.

Above *A corona appears, as the moon shines through thin cloud.*

thin layer of ice crystals such as cirro-stratus, a halo, or colored ring is seen circling the sun or moon. This time, red is on the inside, followed by yellow, green, white and blue on the outside. The colors are rarely distinct though, and the halo usually appears as a dark shadowy inner ring edged by a brighter one. There are also two sizes of haloes, which occur because different ice crystals bend the light to two different degrees. The smaller halo is seen most often, but on rare occasions, the two appear together.

Weather charts and satellites

High and low pressure

The weather charts we see in newspapers and on television, with their high and low pressure areas, show us in a way the hills and valleys of the atmosphere. The lines which circle the areas of pressure are called **isobars,** and they join places of equal pressure. The closer together the isobars, the stronger the wind (which follows the isobars) will be. Because the Earth's rotation deflects the wind, the northern hemisphere winds blow counterclockwise around low pressure and clockwise around the high. In the southern hemisphere the directions are reversed.

Air in a low pressure area (also called a depression) is rising and cooling, which results in clouds and rain. The reverse is true of high pressure, where the air is slowly sinking, warming up and drying out. Low pressure is therefore usually associated with wet or stormy weather, and high pressure with fine dry weather.

The isobars on a weather map show lines of equal pressure, like the contour lines on an ordinary map.

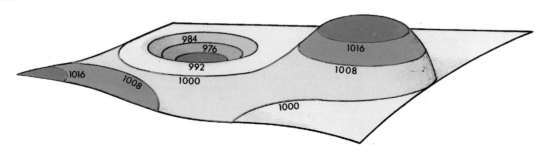

Fronts

The atmosphere is constantly being altered by the surface over which it travels. Air that travels over a warm sea will become warm and humid, while air that remains over land will become dry; and, depending on whether the land is cold or warm, it will warm up or cool down. At any given time therefore, there will be large areas of the atmosphere which are either warm or cold, and the boundaries between these air masses are called **fronts.**

The clearest example of a front is the polar front. (The example that follows describes the northern hemisphere, but it is also true for the southern.) The polar front separates cold polar air from the warmer air to the south. The cold air is trying to go south, while the warm air is trying to go north. If neither is winning, the front is stationary. On a weather map it will be shown as a line with spikes and blobs on alternate sides. But a polar front usually isn't stationary for long; warm air will eventually push north or cold air push south. The front will then develop a kink. Now the front has cold air moving south on one side, and warm air going north on the other. The boundary of the cold front is shown as a line with spikes pointing in the direction of the movement. Similarly the warm

An area of low pressure (marked "L") developing at a polar front.

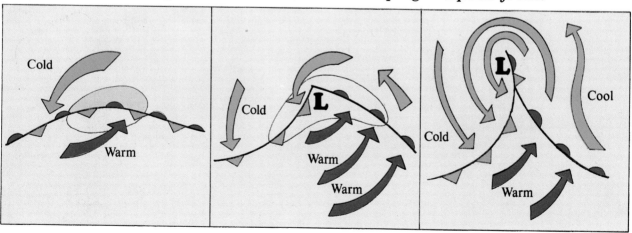

front will have blobs pointing in the direction of movement. Sometimes the kink straightens out, but usually it develops further and a low pressure area forms at the tip. This low may develop further into one of the large depressions that are common in the **latitudes** near the polar front.

Cold fronts move faster than warm fronts and so tend to catch up with them. Also, cold air is heavier and denser, so, as the front advances, the cold air will undercut the warm. Similarly the warm air behind the advancing warm front will rise up on the cold air in front of it, causing clouds and rain to form (see page 30). Eventually, the cold air will lift all the warm air aloft as the cold front catches up with the warm; where this happens the front is said to be occluded and is shown on the map as a line with blobs and spikes on the same side.

Right *A cloud front advances over the Antarctic coast at sunset.*

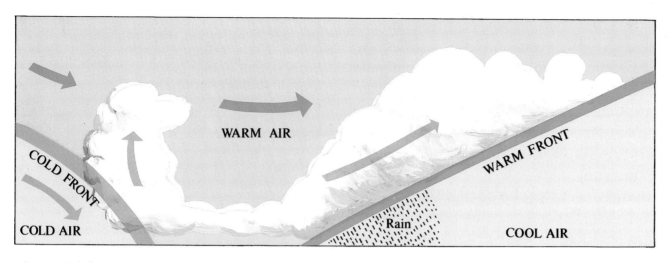

The cold front moves forward, undercutting the warm air.

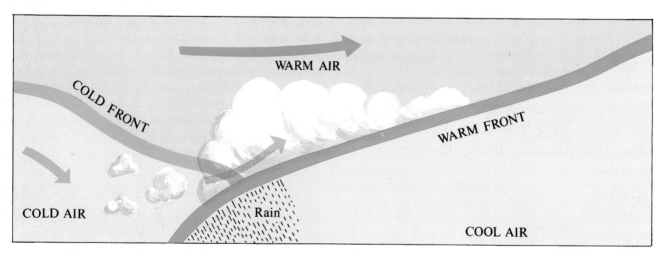

The front then becomes occluded as the cold air forces the cloudy warm air aloft.

Weather satellites

The pictures received from weather satellites orbiting the Earth are an invaluable aid to **meteorologists.** There are two sorts of weather satellites: polar orbiting, and geostationary. The polar orbiting satellites pass near the Earth's poles, hence the name. They orbit the Earth several times each day, which enables them to view the whole globe in the course of twenty-four hours. The geostationary satellites orbit the equator, traveling in the same direction and at the same speed as the Earth spins. Seen from the ground they appear to be stationary in the sky, so they therefore view the same area of the globe continuously.

The satellites take pictures of the Earth, not only in daylight, but also at night with **infrared** cameras. Instead of recording light, the cameras record the different temperatures being emitted by objects—warm areas of land and sea appear dark; high cloud, which is very cold, appears white; and the lower clouds appear in varying shades of gray, depending on their height and temperature. This method makes it easier for the weather forecasters to distinguish between the different types of cloud—and this helps them greatly in their predictions. Weather satellites can also measure the atmosphere's density, its dustiness, and even the concentrations of gases such as water vapor, carbon dioxide and ozone.

Cold cloud appears white on a satellite picture.

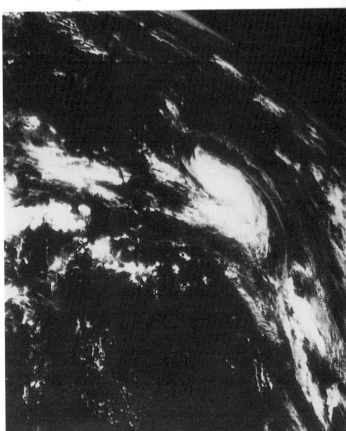

Climate and the atmosphere

Weather is with us all the time, everywhere. In some places it changes every day, in others it remains much the same. "Climate" is the technical term used to describe the average weather of a place—but the period of time over which the average is taken is important. For example, some regions of the world have contrasting winter and summer seasons, so if you averaged the winter weather and compared it with the following summer, you would mistakenly conclude that the climate was getting warmer. In fact, averages are taken over at least thirty-year periods, with winters and summers being averaged separately. But suppose the climate of this region alternates between thirty-year spells of warm winters and summers and thirty-year spells of cold winters and summers. You'd need to average the records for 200 years to find this out, but then you might worry that those 200 years were part of a larger cycle . . . and so on. This goes to show that all too often, sensational newspaper headlines say that our climate is changing when the evidence is very far from conclusive!

Climate not only changes from place to place; it also changes with height. The upper slopes of mountains have very different climates from the lower slopes, mainly because temperature decreases with height. But mountain valleys may be as barren as the upper slopes because cold katabatic winds flowing down the mountain collect in the valleys, forming frost hollows which stunt the vegetation.

Some desert climates are almost permanently dry.

Cold mountain air has stunted the growth of these trees.

Sometimes climate changes dramatically over a relatively short distance. Prevailing winds from the sea rising over a mountainous island will form clouds and rain. For example, the northeast slopes of Hawaii are very wet, but as the humid air descends the other side of the mountains, the air is warmed and dried, so the clouds and rain clear. The southwest of Hawaii therefore has a much drier climate than the northeast.

You might expect that the closer to the poles you go, the colder the climate. But that is only partly true; the climate of the British Isles is mild, while Newfoundland is subarctic—although the British Isles are farther north! This is because a cold ocean current (the Labrador current) sweeps down from the Arctic Ocean, past the eastern coasts of Newfoundland, whereas the British Isles are warmed by the Gulf Stream—an ocean current from the balmy Caribbean.

These examples show how sensitive individual climates are to various factors. Many different factors, such as latitude, the nearness of the sea, prevailing winds, types of vegetation, monsoon winds, mountain ranges and the size of the continents, all contribute to the variety of climates found on Earth. There are far too many to consider here, as any good atlas will show. However, it must be said that even a place with the most settled climate can, on rare occasions, have totally unexpected weather. Death Valley in California (which is normally one of the hottest places on Earth) had snow on January 9, 1937.

The extent of the Arctic ice cap during an ice age.

Ice ages

A study of the global climates of the past reveals that they have alternated between warm and cold over many millions of years. During the cold periods the polar ice sheets and mountain **glaciers** all increased—covering much more of the globe than they do now. These cold periods are therefore known as ice ages.

The last ice age occurred about 20,000 years ago. The ice sheet was on average 800 meters (2,625 feet) thick, and the sites of cities such as Boston, Chicago, Glasgow, Leningrad and Stockholm were completely buried. In some places the ice was as thick as the Greenland and Antarctic ice caps of today (2,500 meters, or 8,200 feet). There was even ice on the tropical mountains. Much of North America, Europe and Russia would have been uninhabitable.

The milder intervals between ice ages are called interglacial periods. They are shorter than ice ages—in fact, it seems that ice ages are normal and interglacials are the exception. The shortest interglacial is only 15,000 years, compared with the shortest ice age of around 60,000 years. Our present interglacial has lasted about 9,000 years.

There are also less dramatic fluctuations in the climate within interglacial periods. For example, the period between 1900 and 1960 was much warmer than the previous few centuries. But around 1940 the northern hemisphere's climate began to cool—but we don't know if this trend is likely to continue. Perhaps we should hope it will, because too long and hot a spell would melt enough ice to raise the sea level significantly!

Climatic change

Climatic change is a complicated process which depends on a combination of changes in ocean temperature, the global amount of cloud, the extent of polar ice, variations in the sun's energy, the position of the Earth's orbit around the sun—and also human activities.

The atmosphere surrounds the Earth like a blanket—trapping the sun's heat while the global winds circulate it evenly. Any change in the atmosphere's composition will undoubtedly affect the climate, but the effect is likely to be unpredictable. For example, clouds reflect sunlight, but they also act like a blanket to retain the Earth's heat—so it is not clear whether more cloud would warm or cool the atmosphere.

Dust will also reduce the amount of sunlight reaching the Earth's surface.

Climatic change might increase the Earth's cloud cover.

The effect could be similar to that of clouds; the atmosphere might cool. But not all dust reflects sunlight. A metallic dust would absorb sunlight and become heated. If enough metallic dust became trapped in the upper atmosphere it would be another heat source, rather like the ozone layer, and the atmosphere would heat up. Little sunlight would penetrate the dust, so conditions would be hazy as well as warm and oppressive —similar to thundery weather.

Large **meteors** vaporizing on entering the Earth's atmosphere are a possible source of metallic dust, but volcanoes are the most likely source of reflective dust. Tambora, a volcano in Indonesia, threw an immense cloud of fine reflective dust into the atmosphere when it erupted in 1815—and the worldwide climate that year was noticeably cooler. In 1980 the eruption of the American volcano, Mount St. Helens, was expected to have similar effects, but the dust fell out of the atmosphere sooner than expected. Because of this, the eruption of the Mexican volcano El Chichón, in March 1982, did not arouse much interest. But the El Chichón eruption was larger than Mount St. Helens, and it was different because, as well as the usual amount of dust, it also ejected enormous amounts of sulfur dioxide gas. The gas reacted with the atmosphere to form a cloud of tiny sulfuric acid droplets. This cloud has since smeared itself through the upper atmosphere as a sunlight thinning veil around the globe. This created much

Mt. St. Helen's, 1980, sending up a massive plume of volcanic ash.

more scientific interest, and the eruption was even called the "Weather-Maker of the Century" in the U.S. weather magazine *Weatherwise*.

Man's effect on the atmosphere

Because of the tiny quantities of ozone and carbon dioxide in the atmosphere, mankind can affect the quantities present quite significantly.

Man-made pollution could affect the Earth's climate.

Most of the ozone in the atmosphere is in a thin layer, where it absorbs some of the sun's energy and so warms the atmosphere. But if chemicals called fluorocarbons find their way into the ozone layer, they react with ultraviolet light from the sun, forming new chemicals, some of which destroy ozone.

37

The main source of fluorocarbons is the aerosol spray can. Some scientists believe these sprays threaten the existence of the ozone layer. Chemicals from the exhaust gases of high-flying aircraft are thought to have a similar effect.

However, the more likely cause of climatic change as a result of Man's activity is the increase of carbon dioxide in the atmosphere. Carbon dioxide is largely transparent to sunshine, but it traps the heat that rises from the warmed Earth. The process is sometimes referred to as the "greenhouse effect" because the glass in a greenhouse has the same effect—allowing the sunshine in, but preventing the accumulated heat from escaping. Most scientists agree that an increased amount of carbon dioxide will warm the atmosphere—but argue as to how much that increase will have to be to affect the climate.

The amount of carbon dioxide in the atmosphere has been increasing steadily since the turn of the century, and it has been estimated that by the year 2000 the concentration would be 30% to 50% higher than it was in 1900. The increase over the last few decades has been mainly due to the increased use of fossil fuels (coal and oil).

Also, **deforestation** leads indirectly to an increase in carbon dioxide levels, as vegetation uses up carbon dioxide—in effect breathing it in, and breathing out oxygen. The tropical rain forests are currently being irresponsibly destroyed at the rate of 50 acres a minute. If this continues there will be no rain forest left by the end of this century.

To stop the increase of carbon dioxide will require more energy conservation and the development of alternative energy sources, other than fossil fuels. Planting more forests and protecting those that remain are also essential, and perhaps vital.

Right *The annual orbit of the Earth around the sun creates the seasons.*

The Earth's orbit

The Earth spins on its **axis** once every twenty-four hours—giving us our day and night. As well as turning on its axis, the Earth orbits the sun once a year. This orbit is not quite a circle; at certain times of the year the Earth is closer to the sun than at others.

Also, the Earth's axis is tilted 23.5°

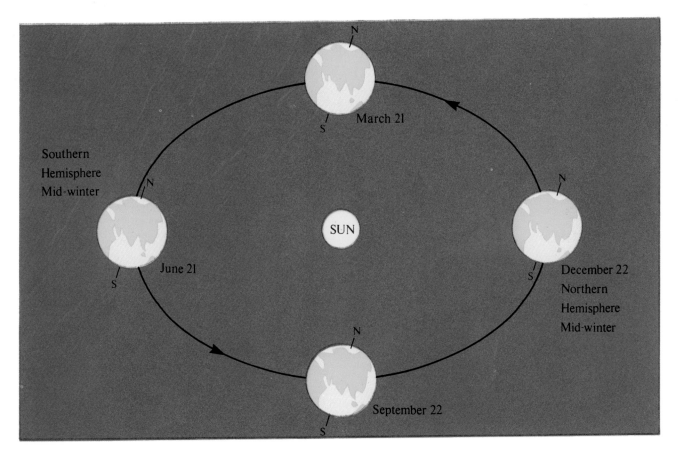

from the vertical, and it is this tilt which gives the seasons. During winter in the northern hemisphere, the axis is tilted away from the sun, and so the sun is lower in the sky than in summer. Because the sun is lower in the sky in winter it spends less time above the horizon, and so the days are shorter. Also, in winter the sun's rays must pass through more atmosphere, so they lose more of their energy. The weakness of

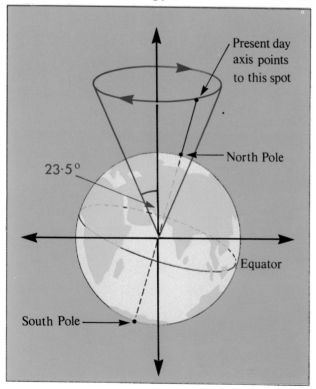

Present day axis points to this spot

North Pole

23·5°

Equator

South Pole

the sun's rays, combined with the shorter day, makes winter colder than summer.

But while the northern hemisphere freezes in winter, the southern hemisphere enjoys summer. If the Earth's axis tilted the other way the seasons would be reversed—midsummer in the northern hemisphere would be in December. But then midsummer would occur when the Earth was at its closest to the sun, and midwinter when it was at its farthest. Temperature extremes between winter and summer in the north would therefore be more severe than they are now, and the Earth's climate less hospitable.

Precession

As the Earth spins in space, its axis "points" to a particular position in the sky. This position slowly changes in a circular pattern, which repeats itself every 26,000 years. This is called **precession.** One of the most popular theories as to the cause of ice ages is that they are caused by precession. Ice ages caused in this way would start and finish fairly gradually. However, well-

The Earth's axis also revolves.

preserved, frozen mammoths have been found in Siberia—which might suggest that ice ages started suddenly.

Not only changes in the tilt of the Earth's axis affect climate. Changes in the Earth's orbit will also do so. Gravity keeps the Earth and all the other planets circling the sun at different speeds; the planets nearer the sun circle faster than those further away. Also, all the planets affect each other's orbits by their own gravitational pull. At intervals of about 180 years, the larger and farther planets group themselves on one side of the sun. (This last happened in 1982.) According to some Chinese scientists, the Earth will be speeded up slightly as it approaches the grouping of larger planets, because of the combined gravitational pull of the grouping. The same effect should likewise slow the Earth down as it moves away from the grouping. The overall effect would be to make the northern hemisphere winters longer and the summers shorter (and vice versa in the southern hemisphere). There seems to be some evidence to support the theory, because for the past thirty years the climate of New Zealand seems to have been warming up. However, the evidence is still being examined, and many scientists have yet to be convinced.

Weather and climate on other planets

It is interesting to look at some of the other planets in the solar system, and compare their weather and climate to those of the Earth.

Jupiter's axis only tilts about 3°, so it has virtually no seasons. At the other extreme, the axis of Uranus is inclined nearly in line with the sun. This has the odd effect of there being only one day and night in its year. It could also be said that Uranus's summer is its day, and the winter its night.

We know much more about the Earth's neighbors, Mars and Venus, as they have been visited by U.S. and Russian space probes. Mars is farther from the sun than Earth, and is therefore colder. The atmosphere is mainly carbon dioxide, but there is a small amount of water vapor. The planet is desertlike, and with a thin, scarce atmosphere and no oceans to circulate the sun's heat evenly, the contrast between day and

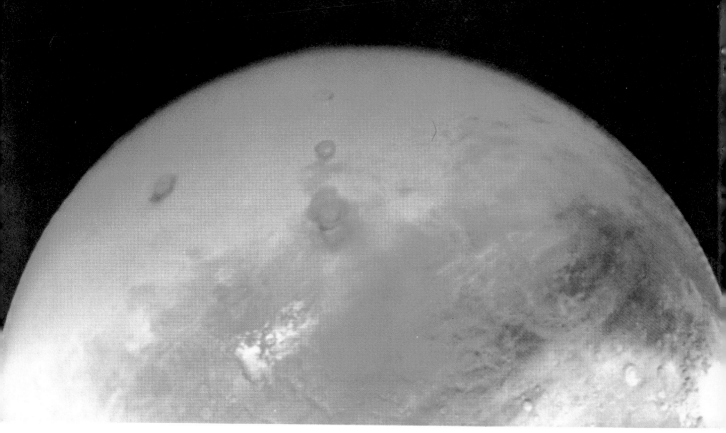

The surface of Mars is often obscured by enormous dust storms.

night temperatures is large. On average, the maximum day temperature might be -20°C (-4°F) and the minimum at night -70°C (-94°F). An Earth desert would usually only range between 40°C (140°F) and 20°C (68°F). The weather on Mars includes features found on Earth; it has clouds, low pressure areas, and what appear to be cold fronts. However, the most spectacular feature is the great Martian dust storm. This storm

is similar to a hurricane, and is believed to form when a cloud of dust in the atmosphere becomes heated by the sun. The dustcloud in turn heats the atmosphere, and more dust is raised into the atmosphere by convection. This extra dust then heats up . . . and so on until storm winds are generated. After about six weeks, the entire planet is obscured by dust. The storm then takes from fifteen to twenty-five weeks to die down.

Venus is closer to the sun, and in contrast to Mars, is always totally obscured by thick cloud. Recent space probes revealed that the atmosphere is astonishingly dense, and almost completely (96%) composed of carbon dioxide. The Venusian atmosphere is therefore a very warm blanket indeed. The surface temperature is around 480°C (896°F) and doesn't vary much. Because of its slow rotation, Venus also has a very long day and night (243 Earth days), and also no high or low pressure areas, which would require a much faster rotation to develop. The clouds are composed of extremely corrosive acid droplets. The clouds lie in several layers, but their acid raindrops probably evaporate in the intense heat long before they reach the surface. Despite the heat, very little sun can penetrate the cloud, so daylight is always a gloomy red glow. All in all, we can see that the other planets have extremely inhospitable climates compared with that of the Earth.

Only Earth has a hospitable climate.

Facts and figures

"Supertyphoons" occur over the China Sea. They can be as large as the whole United States, and release more energy than the first atomic bomb.

The habit of giving exotic names to hurricanes was started in Australia at the turn of the century. In recent years, both Australia and America have used boys' and girls' names alternately. The names allocated to the Atlantic hurricanes of 1983 were: Alicia, Barry, Chantal, Dean, Erin, Felix, Gabrielle, Hugo, Iris, Jerry, Karen, Luis, Marylin, Noel, Opal, Pablo, Roxanne, Sebastien, Tanya, Van, and Wendy.

The strongest tornadoes will hurl railway locomotives and whole houses some distance.

A mild tornado will remove chimney pots and uproot small trees. Hurricane Beulah (September 1967) was estimated to have "given birth" to as many as 115 tornadoes.

There are case histories of tornadoes having occurred in Australia, Bangladesh, Belgium, Canada, Great Britain, Italy, and New Zealand.

If all the world's ice melted, the sea level would probably rise by about 80 meters (262 feet)—and drown many of the world's major cities.

On average, there are thunderstorms in Java on 322 days each year.

In 1971, rain fell on the desert of Atacama in Chile—the first time in 400 years.

Further reading

Alth, Max and Alth, Charlotte. *Disastrous Hurricanes and Tornadoes*. New York: Franklin Watts, 1981.

Berger, Melvin. *Disastrous Floods and Tidal Waves*. New York: Franklin Watts, 1981.

Cohen, Daniel. *What's Happening to Our Weather?* New York: M. Evans, 1979.

Ford, Adam. *Weather Watch*. New York: Lothrop, Lee and Shepard, 1982.

Gilfond, Henry. *The New Ice Age*. New York: Franklin Watts, 1978.

Lampton, Christopher. *Meteorology: An Introduction*. New York: Franklin Watts, 1981.

National Geographic. *An Introduction to Weather*. Washington, DC: National Geographic, 1981.

Pringle, Laurence. *Frost Hollows and Other Microclimates*. New York: William Morrow, 1981.

Simon, Seymour. *Weather and Climate*. New York: Random House, 1969.

Glossary

Anabatic winds   These are also called upslope winds. They develop when warm air rises from the sunny slopes of hills on calm days.

Axis   An imaginary line about which a spinning object (such as the Earth) rotates.

Convection   A circulation in a liquid or gas, caused by heating.

Cumulus   Lumpy, cauliflower shaped clouds formed by convecton.

Deforestation   The deliberate destruction of trees and other vegetation on a large scale, often for cultivating crops or for building.

Dewpoint   The temperature at which water vapor in the air starts to change (condense) into water.

Equator   An imaginary line circling the earth, that separates the northern from the southern hemisphere.

Evaporation   The process by which a liquid becomes a vapor. For example, water evaporates and becomes water vapor.

Fronts   Air masses frequently have very different characteristics: cold or warm, or moist or dry. The boundary between such air masses is a front.

Glaciers   Very slowly flowing rivers of ice.

Gravity   The force of attraction that every object possesses. The more massive the object, the greater the gravitational pull. A stone falls to the ground because of the pull of Earth's gravity.

High pressure areas (anticyclones)   The more atmosphere there is over a place the higher will be the pressure at that place. Often an excess of air will accumulate over a large area forming a "hill" of air (high pressure). The air within the hill will gently flow downwards, becoming warm and dry as it does so. The Earth's rotation deflects the flowing air, clockwise in the northern hemisphere, and counterclockwise in the southern.

Infrared radiation   Our eyes can only see certain wavelengths of radiation, red light being the lowest. Below this wavelength is infrared, which we cannot see, but which is actually heat. Infrared cameras are sensitive to this infrared radiation—in other words, to the heat emitted by objects.

Isobars   The lines on a weather chart, which are drawn through places that have the same atmospheric pressure. The wind tends to blow parallel with, or to follow along the isobars, and the closer together the isobars, the stronger the wind.

Katabatic winds   These are sometimes called downslope winds. They develop when cold air flows downhill, usually overnight when the air is cooled by the cold ground.

Latitudes   Imaginary horizontal lines circling the Earth, parallel to the equator. They are measured in degrees north or south of the equator, i.e. the equator is 0°, the North Pole is 90° north of the equator, and the South Pole is 90° south.

Low pressure areas (depressions)   Just as high pressure areas are the "hills" of the atmosphere, low pressure areas are the "valleys". Low pressure develops when more air flows out of a region than flows into it. The air in such a region tries to flow toward the center of low pressure, but is deflected by the Earth's rotation—counterclockwise in the northern hemisphere, and clockwise in the southern.

Meteors   Lumps of material from outer space. Usually they are small and burn up as they hit the atmosphere (so-called "shooting stars".) Meteors large enough to reach the Earth's surface are called meteorites.

Molecule   A very minute particle formed when smaller particles (atoms) cluster together. A molecule of water is formed of two atoms of hydrogen and one of oxygen.

Monsoon   A seasonal wind affecting a huge area. It is caused by temperature differences between a continental land mass and the ocean.

Ozone layer   A layer of air 50 kilometers (30 miles) above the Earth's surface, which has a high concentration of ozone.

Precession   The Earth's axis "points" to a particular position in the sky. The position slowly changes in a circular motion, and this change is known as precession.

Precipitation   A general description of what can fall from clouds. Rain, hail, drizzle, snow and sleet are all forms of precipitation.

Refraction   Light, on entering a transparent substance such as glass or water, will be bent or refracted. White light is composed of all the colors of the spectrum, each color being bent at a slightly different angle, which is why white light on entering a glass block or prism is split into the separate colors of the spectrum.

Spectrum   The seven colors of the spectrum which compose white light: red, orange, yellow, green, blue, indigo, and violet.

Stratosphere   The second layer of the atmosphere, above the troposphere.

Stratus   A sheet of low cloud. When stratus lies on the ground it is usually known as fog.

Thermals   Bubbles of warm air rising from the sun-warmed ground.

Tornadoes   Small, intense whirling tubes of wind, attached to a dark, funnel-shaped cloud. The highest wind speeds of all are found in tornadoes.

Troposphere   The layer of atmosphere nearest the Earth's surface, where the weather takes place. The word means "sphere of change".

Typhoons   The local name for hurricanes originating in the China Sea.

Ultraviolet radiation   Infrared describes radiation wavelengths *below* visible light. Ultraviolet describes wavelengths *beyond* the violet end of the visible light spectrum. Ultraviolet radiation from the sun would be harmful to us but fortunately, the ozone layer filters most of it out before it reaches the Earth's surface.

Index

Picture acknowledgments

From Bruce Coleman Limited: Jen and Des Bartlett 30, B. and C. Calhoun 20, Robert P. Carr 14, Jeff Foott *front cover*, 16, 25, C. B. Frith 18 (below), Carol Hughes 23, John Pearson 35; GeoScience Features Picture Library 9, 18 (above), 19 (above and below), 22, 24, 32, 33, 43; HMSO Crown Copyright 13, 17; from the Meteorological Office: S. D. Burt 26, R. N. Hughes 26, P. J. May 15; NASA 6, 7, 13, 31, 42; Wayland Picture Library 4, 5, 8, 37; Zefa 21. The diagrams on pages 10, 11, 12, 27, 28, 30, 34, 39, and 40 are by Malcolm S. Walker.